UPON HIGH PLACES
Stories from the mountains of Wales

Upon High Places

Stories from the mountains of Wales

Mike Perrin

Gwasg **Bryntirion** Press

© Mike Perrin
First published 1997
ISBN 1 85049 133 X

Unless otherwise indicated, Scripture quotations are from the
Holy Bible, New International Version (1984),
used by permission of Hodder and Stoughton Ltd.

Cover photograph: Dave Newbould
Cover design: burgum boorman ltd.

Published by
Gwasg **Bryntirion** Press
(formerly Evangelical Press of Wales)
Bryntirion, Bridgend CF31 4DX, Wales, UK
Printed and bound by Creative Print and Design (Wales), Ebbw Vale

Contents

In memory of Carl whose love for the
mountains of Eryri and Ethiopia has now been
replaced by unbroken joy on the heights
of Emmanuel's land

Then shalt thou delight thyself in the Lord; and I will cause thee
*to ride **upon the high places** of the earth, and feed thee with the heritage of Jacob*
thy father: for the mouth of the Lord hath spoken it.
(Isaiah 58:14 AV)

Introduction

Both the first and the final chapters of this book were written some while before any thought of writing additional material for publication was ever seriously contemplated. These chapters relate to two significant events in our life during the course of which thoughts and feelings arose which I wanted very much to commit to paper. Though this was done primarily for very personal reasons, one or two friends who read them encouraged me to consider writing in a similar way about other experiences or events which might be a challenge or an encouragement to others. That these additional chapters should have a common theme of mountains and that the title *Upon High Places* should be chosen for this small work is hardly surprising. Hills and mountains have always had a powerful influence upon my life. From Exmoor and Dartmoor in childhood to Scotland, the Alps, Corsica and the Pyrenees in later life, I have never been happier than when in remote and lofty places. I would avidly read books of travel and mountain adventure as a youngster. In 1953 when the nation was preoccupied with the Coronation, I could think of little else but my heroes descending Everest after their triumphant conquest of the world's highest mountain.

But it must surely be the many years it has been our privilege to live and work in North Wales, that has constituted the greatest influence of all. Our first home in Gwynedd, Hafod Wydyr, was situated at the very foot of Yr Wyddfa (or Snowdon as some prefer to call it), and whilst we now live on the coast we can still see that most beautiful of Welsh peaks from our front door. The ten exciting years we were involved in the work of the Christian Mountain Centre took us into the hills almost daily, while the joy experienced by the many hundreds of young people we introduced to the mountains only added to our own deep appreciation of and love for such high places.

People frequently asked at that time what it was that had caused such a rugged landscape (and very often a wet one, too!) to mean so much to us. Usually my reply was that Jesus clearly had a deep affinity with the hills. What could be more natural then that some of his followers share that love? Indeed, when challenged on occasions to justify the setting-up of a Christian Mountain Centre, we loved to quote Mark 3:13,14, 'Jesus went up into the hills and called to him those he wanted, and they came to him . . . that they might be with him and that he might send them out'. To us, those verses enshrined the *raison d'être* for the Centre's existence—Jesus in the mountains, calling to himself those whom he desired, that they might live with him and go out to work for him. Small wonder, that those of us who were called to live and serve him in this way were always so aware of his presence with us as we walked upon those high places.

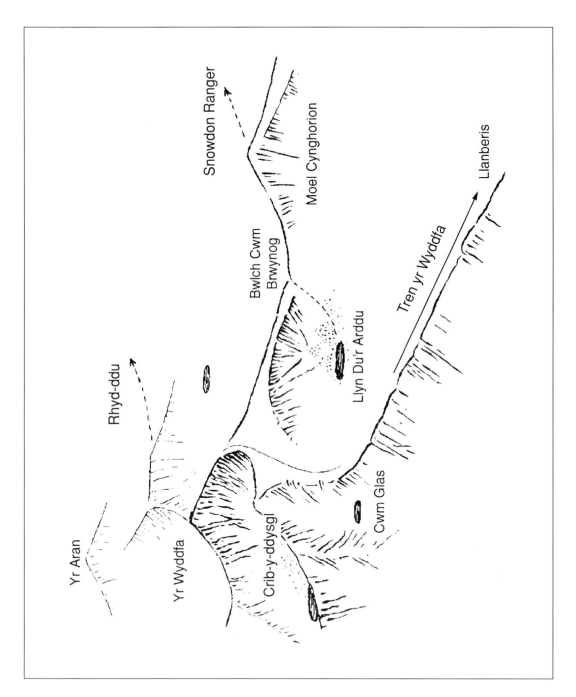

The Snowdon (Yr Wyddfa) area

1
Night on the Mountain

'Surely the Lord is in this.' (Genesis 28:10-21)

From high on the hillside above, only the occasional bleat of a sheep broke the silence of the night. A gust of wind rustled some rushes nearby. I shivered, drew the hood of my sleeping-bag a little tighter and lay there looking up at a host of stars. With no rain for several weeks the ground was hard and my boots did not make the most comfortable pillow, but in that moment there was nowhere I would rather be. The steep cliff of Clogwyn Du'r Arddu rose from the scree on the far side of the small lake. Those who had ascended Yr Wyddfa (Snowdon) by track or by train in their hundreds during the day, had long since returned to their comforts in the valley below. Now, for these few hours of darkness, the high places were mine to appreciate alone.

What had prompted such strange behaviour? My own home and a warm bed were but ten miles away. What makes someone of 'mature' years voluntarily exchange such comfort for a bivouac under the stars? I might reply, a deep and lifelong love of the mountains, but that would only be part of the truth. For I felt the need to take stock of the situation I now found myself in, and for me that required time in a silent and solitary place. The blessings of comfort and companionship can sometimes cloud the mind. I needed to see things clearly.

Three years before, almost to the day, our dear son Carl had been drowned in the swollen floodwaters of the River Cothi in Dyfed. He was only twenty-eight. He had been serving God as a water-engineer in Ethiopia for several years firstly with Tear[1] Fund and then with SIM[2]. Then so suddenly, whilst visiting his family and friends, God chose to take him 'home'. How we missed him and grieved his loss.

Before another year had run its course, my wife Elaine was diagnosed as having a brain tumour and was immediately admitted to the Royal London Hospital for treatment. God saw fit to spare her and months of anxious waiting and wondering gave way to a programme of rehabilitation, but this experience also served to remind us of human fragility and the uncertainty of our days.

And now, while perhaps we were still learning to come to terms with these experiences, we faced a third crisis. It had sadly become necessary to resign as pastor and leave the Baptist church in Colchester it had been such a joy and privilege to serve. I began to suffer from a persistent asthma-related cough soon after accepting the call to the church. Now, after seven years of ministry amongst a people we had grown to love, I had at last been forced to give up. Medical opinion was unanimous: the coughing had so affected my voice that were I to remain in Essex and continue preaching, the larynx would be irreversibly damaged and complete voice loss would result within a year. It was a most painful decision to take, but we had to accept that this must be the will of God. We had lived in North Wales for 23 years before we ever moved to Colchester; we still had a house near Porthmadog, with a church and people we knew well close by—surely God was saying that we should return to our former home.

As we moved back to Wales there may well have been some who envied us. It all seemed so simple—early retirement in a beautiful part of the country; more time to spend with our grandchildren; the opportunity to pursue one's hobbies, and so on. But as I lay 'cocooned' in my sleeping-bag looking up at the night sky,

[1] The Evangelical Alliance Relief Fund
[2] Society for International Ministries, formerly the Sudan Interior Mission

my mind was being assailed by other thoughts. Why was it God had brought us to this situation? Whatever did the future hold? Could I really accept the possibility of never preaching on a regular basis again, particularly when preaching the gospel had always meant so much to me? And what about the small matter of financial provision? I thanked God for our home, but would State benefit be sufficient to live on? All this was unknown territory. I'd not been here before, and the confused nature of my thinking bore testimony to my sense of perplexity.

Then it was I remembered Jacob. What turbulent thoughts he must have had as he trekked northwards from Beersheba toward Haran. He must have been afraid because his brother Esau had threatened to kill him. And he may well have had a sense of past failure and possibly a feeling of guilt. He is also likely to have been acutely aware of his own frailty as he set out alone on a walk of over four hundred miles across largely trackless wilderness. And what would he find at the end of his journey? What sort of a future could he look forward to? Somehow my own needs began to appear quite insignificant beside those of Jacob, but still I followed him in my mind. My climbing boots must have been quite comfortable compared with the stone he chose for a pillow as darkness fell. Weary from his walking, however, he slept and, sleeping, he dreamed. But his was no ordinary dream made up of senseless fragments which become even more meaningless when you try to remember them the following morning. Jacob's dream was God-given revelation and as vivid as if he were observing reality with wide-open eyes and a fully conscious mind.

There are two elements to Jacob's vision described in Genesis 28:12,13. It is questionable whether the better known and more frequently remembered of the two is really the more important. The ladder or stairway between heaven and earth, with angels ascending and descending, certainly has much to say to those who are trying to make sense of the confused events of their lives. Jacob's ladder is there to remind us that earth and heaven—the realms of the material and the spiritual—are not totally separated, the one unreachable from the other. There is a place where the gulf that normally divides the two can be bridged. The heartfelt cry or fervent prayer of a person, even of Jacob's reputation, can ascend and be heard in heaven's throne-room. At the same time, an unlimited supply of forgiveness, mercy and strength is forever being despatched from on high and is thus freely available to those below who feel their need of such gracious provision. What hope and refreshment such a picture gives to the weary traveller on life's journey!

And yet there is an even more glorious (though frequently overlooked) truth revealed to Jacob, and one that brought even greater comfort to my own heart that night on the mountainside. According to Genesis 28:13, *there above . . . stood the Lord.* Angels ascending and descending must have been something to behold, but not even this could rival the sight of the glory and majesty of God himself as he stood over all.

From my earliest years I had been taught to believe that God is sovereign and reigns both in heaven and earth; that he is in perfect control of the affairs of nations and individuals, and that he had a plan for my life. From the day I began in Christian ministry I had sought to teach this glorious fact. *We know that all things work together for good to those who love God, to those who are called according to his purpose . . . If God is for us, who can be against us? . . . In all (these) things we are more than conquerors through him who loved us . . . Oh, the depth of the riches both of the wisdom and knowledge of God! How unsearchable are his judgments and his ways past finding out! For who has known the mind of the Lord? Or who has become his counsellor? . . . For of him and through him and to him are all things, to whom be glory forever* (Romans 8:28,31,37; 11:33,34,36 NKJV).

But truth—even glorious truth—however clearly understood in the mind and embraced by faith in the heart, needs to be applied to daily circumstances and personal experience. And this is sometimes the hardest part of all.

In my bivouac below Clogwyn Du'r Arddu on Snowdon I dreamed no dream (of any relevance) nor saw any vision. As I gazed at the night sky, however, trying to comprehend the vastness of space; as I marvelled at the sheer number of stars and galaxies visible to the naked eye, recognising that man could see unaided only a tiny part of an incomprehensibly vast universe, so the sublime realisation dawned—my Father in heaven created all of this! *He made the stars also* may have been a simple statement of fact recorded in Genesis 1:16 AV, but for those who have been brought by grace into the family of God, what implications! The mighty Lord of creation who flung the stars into space and who keeps the planets in their orbit is also the Father who loved me enough to send his Son to die for me, and that being so—*He who did not spare his own Son, but delivered him up for us all, how shall he not with him also freely give us all things?* (Romans 8:32 NKJV). God really was in control of the situation. He had the power and authority to order all things according to his wise and loving counsels. All that had happened from the moment of my birth, he not only knew about but had divinely controlled for my good and his glory. Why should I be perplexed or anxious? How could I possibly fear the future? Did it really matter if my role or ministry amongst his people were to change or that I might not preach regularly again? He had saved me not to be a preacher but to be his child. All he required of me was that I should trust him. And with that I slept.

I awoke at 5 o'clock, rolled up my sleeping-bag and was on the summit of Snowdon in time to see the sunrise. A new day had begun.

The Outside Edge on Craig Cwm Silyn

2
Rock Climbing

'He will not let your foot slip.' (Psalm 121:3)

An elderly couple parked their car by the roadside below Tremadog cliffs and stood watching the diminutive figures of three climbers negotiating the overhanging rock face which reared up above the trees. 'Why are they tied together with ropes?' enquired the wife. 'Dunno really,' responded her husband. 'Something to do with British "team-spirit" I wouldn't wonder—one falls off, they all fall off!' Black humour? Cynicism? Or simply a total inability, shared by so many, to even begin to understand why anyone should ever want to do such a thing and how they can possibly safeguard themselves as they do it.

It hardly needs to be said that rock climbing, especially at an advanced level, looks dangerous. For some who participate this may be part of the attraction. They may feel the need to project a 'macho' image. But the fact of the matter is that far more people die from heart-attacks or hypothermia while walking on our hills, than are actually killed in climbing accidents. Very sadly one Christian friend of mine did die when he was rock-climbing even though he was a very competent climber, as did another many years ago at Bible College during a game of rugby. Boating, swimming, skiing or cycling all carry an element of risk and will from time to time claim lives. Yet how dull life would be, particularly for the young, if all such activities were avoided because of the element of risk they involved. How much better to enjoy the challenge of such

17

Mynydd
Tal-y-mignedd

Craig Cwm Silyn

Y Garnedd Goch

'Great Slab'

Llynnau Cwm Silyn

Pen-y-groes

Position of the 'Great Slab'

adventurous pursuits having recognised their dangers and then learned the necessary skills to minimise the risks.

However much our personal circumstances or social standing may differ one from another, and regardless of the extent to which parents or guardians may have sought to provide for us and protect us when we were young and particularly vulnerable, life from its beginning to its end can be seen as a challenging adventure, a journey of exploration and discovery. It is also fraught with danger. Total security against misfortune can never be guaranteed. Even with the greatest privileges and the finest education, 'success' (however that is to be defined) is never certain. The best we can do is to assess the risk, identify the pitfalls and problems that others have encountered, and then recognise those principles and provisions set out by God in his Word, the Bible, which are intended to furnish us with all necessary wisdom, strength and skill. How we react to crisis or cope with hardship will not be determined by the school we attended or how other people perceive us. What *does* matter and is of greatest importance is our readiness to prepare for any and every eventuality by looking to God and asking him to equip us with all that we need not just to survive, but to achieve fully our life's objective as perceived and planned by him.

Just four months after my 'forced' retirement and return to Wales, I was walking with a friend in Cwm Silyn. Many years earlier Paul and I had been students together, and in the years that followed we were to share many enjoyable hours walking and climbing together in the mountains. Now, however, the years were beginning to have an effect, and frequently we paused for breath as we made our way up the huge stone-shoot which fans out from the foot of the gully between Clogwyn y Cysgod and Craig yr Ogof. Eventually we drew level with the Great Slab—a wall of relatively smooth rock rising two hundred feet in height and no more than fifteen degrees off vertical.

What memories that imposing cliff evoked! Much of the climbing here had been pioneered by the great Colin F. Kirkus before the last war, but my mind focused on a day in 1967 when I first climbed a route named 'Outside Edge' (graded V. Diff.). My partner was already familiar with the climb, and I was perfectly happy to follow his lead. Technically the ascent was straightforward enough. In fact, the first one hundred and fifty feet or so followed a natural fault line in the rock which formed a series of linked ledges rising from bottom right to top left across the face of the slab. The 'surprise' came when you reached the edge of the slab and stepped out left onto the 'nose' of the buttress. After climbing a vertical distance of little more than one hundred feet, I found myself looking down between my feet at the tranquil waters of Llynnau Cwm Silyn over six hundred feet below! Four hundred feet of scree sloping down from the base of the buttress to the lake were invisible from my 'eagle's perch' on the protruding nose of rock.

There was an immediate rush of adrenaline and the heart pounded not in fear but with sheer joy and exhilaration! Six hundred feet of space beneath my boots, but my hands and feet were on firm holds whilst the rope, though not tight, ran reassuringly to my leader securely anchored to a belay point some thirty feet above.

Safely negotiating a steep rock face and finding fulfilment in God's plan for your life may not, on the surface, appear to have much in common. Yet it could be said that the same three principles or 'golden rules' need to be applied to both, to ensure complete security and success. We might describe them as the three 'R's of **relationship, reassurance and responsibility**.

I have never been attracted to solo climbing. I concede there are those who, having climbed the very hardest routes roped to a companion, then go on to feel the need to put their skill, strength and courage to the ultimate test by climbing alone. The late Alison Hargreaves found that she climbed better and enjoyed a far greater sense of freedom even on major alpine routes, when she was on her own. (It might also be recalled that when she tragically lost her life in 1995 while descending from the summit of K2, she appears to have been roped to companions.) But this is not the time or place to add to such a long-running debate. Speaking for myself I can only say that much of the pleasure I have known whilst rock-climbing has come from the fact that someone I knew and trusted was at the other end of the rope. Someone with whom I could share the excitement, discuss technique or argue about the correct route, but who above all would protect each difficult move I had to make and provide me with some security should I make a mistake and slip. Rock climbing is all to do with two or more people who can trust and rely upon each other, and whose **relationship** is typified by the rope that joins them together.

In real terms you may not know the other person all that well nor associate with them in other walks of life. Indeed, I have climbed with folk in Scotland and the Alps who were virtual strangers! The only thing I knew about them was that they were competent to attempt the route we both wanted to climb (and that is worth checking out!). But once we both tied on the same rope and started to climb, each became to the other the most important person in the world and remained so for the duration of the ascent. Such a bond is a good illustration of the union described in the Bible between the Lord Jesus Christ and the Christian believer. In John 10:3,4 Jesus describes himself in terms of a good shepherd who *calls his own sheep by name and leads them out*, one who *goes ahead of them* and *whom the sheep follow*. In John 15, however, the relationship represents an even closer association. The shepherd leading with the sheep following now becomes: *I am the vine; you are the branches. If a man remains in me and I in him, he will bear much fruit; apart from me you can do nothing* (John 15:5 NIV). Not some 'marriage of convenience' or expression of mutual respect, but a living and life-giving union in which one is committed totally and for ever to the other and both work together.

Such a relationship at once gives rise to a sense of **reassurance.** In the story I have narrated, I was thrilled rather than terrified by the degree of exposure on Craig Cwm Silyn because the rope to which I was attached, and which had a breaking-strain of over two tons, was being held in such a way that even had I slipped, a fall of no more than three or four inches would have resulted. The whole essence of proper rope management when climbing, is that only one person ever moves at a time. As he or she does so, the rope clipped to the climber's harness is taken in or paid out (usually via a mechanical braking device) by a colleague who is securely anchored or 'belayed' to the rock. Only when the moving climber reaches a safe position and becomes attached to the same or a similar belay point, will the one who has been protecting them put down the rope and prepare to climb themselves.

Those who enter into a personal and living relationship with Christ also have their security assured, but theirs rests not in the strength of any rope but rather in an agreement entered into by God the Father and his Son Jesus Christ. Jesus said, *My sheep listen to my voice; I know them, and they follow me. I give them eternal life, and they shall never perish; no one can snatch them out of my hand. My Father, who has given them to me, is greater than all; no one can snatch them out of my Father's hand* (John 10:27-29). Well might the psalmist say, *He will not let your foot slip . . . The Lord will keep you from all harm—he will watch over your life; the Lord will watch over your coming and going both now and for evermore* (Psalm 121:3,7,8).

But doesn't all this make things just a little too easy? 'Let go and let God' might well seem to be a natural reaction to such a message. If he holds me secure on his 'rope', why not simply lie back and leave it all to him? Your climbing companion would soon have something to say if you opted for such a strategy half-way up a rock face! This is where **responsibility** comes into the equation. In John 10, whilst it is exclusively the shepherd who does the leading, providing and protecting, the sheep are clearly expected to respond and act in a responsible manner. They are to follow (verse 4); run away from 'strangers' (verse 5); listen to the shepherd's voice (verses 16, 27) and believe what he tells them (verse 26). The climbing rope was never introduced to haul a lazy or unwilling participant up a crag like a sack of potatoes! While it is employed to arrest a fall, even novices on their very first climb must climb with care. They must be attentive to what the leader is doing and saying. They must overcome that initial feeling of fear and be resolute and determined to reach the top. All of which Christ surely requires of those who would accept his leadership and follow in his footsteps.

A few weeks after my first ascent of 'Outside Edge' (in the years that followed I returned on a number of occasions to lead others up the same route) a small group of climbers made their way to the foot of Craig Cwm Silyn carrying a stretcher and a body-bag. A young man had been trying to impress his friends by scaling the route alone and had fallen to his death. Tragic, and all the more so, since with a partner and a rope it need never have happened.

3
Abseiling

'Surely God is my salvation; I will trust and not be afraid.' (Isaiah 12:2)

Abseiling is the technique used to descend a rope, the speed of descent being controlled by friction between the rope and the climber's body or some form of abseil device.

(*The Handbook of Climbing*—British Mountaineering Council)

Although my active involvement in the work of the Christian Mountain Centre ended as long ago as 1975, I still enjoy walking to the upper tier of Bwlch Moch, the training crag above Tremadog where those attending courses are introduced to rock-climbing and abseiling. Indeed, when the sun warms the rough-textured rock and I feel sufficiently agile, I may well climb some of the easier routes, and on occasions have even been known to take a rope with me in order to experience yet again the sheer exhilaration of the abseil.

On one occasion three trained instructors from the Mountain Centre were at Bwlch Moch with a group of children and staff from the local secondary school. Climbing up by a route they were not using, I reached the top of the outcrop close to a point from which some of the children had been learning to abseil. The instructor was still there together with a teacher from the school; both were endeavouring to console a tearful twelve-year-old lad. Aled was a pupil with special needs and the teacher present was specifically trained to help such a child. No pressure was being put upon him to abseil down the rock face, which can be intimidating enough for anybody doing it for the very first time.

He didn't *have* to do it. He had been given the option of descending by an easy path to one side of the cliff. The cause of his distress was that he desperately *wanted* to do it. All his friends had gone down at least once, some more than once, and were now at the bottom watching and waiting for him to follow. More than anything else in the world he wanted to do as they had done, but it was that initial step backward over the edge that he found so difficult. Several times he had stood in position facing the instructor who held him securely on a safety rope, but on each occasion a wave of fear had caused him to freeze and the tears of frustration and failure flowed. Did he want to try it one last time? Would he rather go down by way of the path? My own sudden appearance interrupted the discussion, but it also opened up a third option. I looked at the lad as he stood there drying his eyes. 'Aled, I have a rope here just like you are using', I told him. 'If I fixed it alongside yours, would you come down beside me? I'd enjoy your company.' He looked at me and then at the instructor nodding encouragingly. 'OK' was his reply, albeit in a voice that betrayed lingering apprehension.

With my own rope running down the cliff no more than a metre from his, Aled and I stood side by side and slowly leant backwards over the void. Painfully slowly to begin with but with growing confidence in the security of the rope and the rough texture of the rock, we inched our way down the face. Constantly I watched and encouraged him with words of advice and re-assurance. By now we had reached the mid-way point where a narrow ledge ran across that section of the cliff. Noticing that he had been gripping the rope rather tightly I asked Aled if he wanted to rest for a moment. By standing on the ledge some of his weight would be taken off the rope and tense muscles allowed to recover. 'How are you finding it, Aled?' I asked. He looked straight at me. Then his face beamed with the broadest smile imaginable. 'It's just GREAT!' he answered, and I had no cause to doubt his word. Such was his confidence by now, that we came down the final section in a series of bounds allowing the friction device on our harnesses to control the rate of descent. Aled's final jump on to level ground was greeted by wild but nevertheless genuine cheering from his classmates. 'Well done, Aled—you've done it!' was their cry. 'Can I do it again?' was Aled's response!

What valuable lessons can be learnt from this story! How frequently, for example, fear renders a person quite unable to function in the way they would or should! It can have the effect of paralysing an individual so that however much they may want to do something, they find themselves rooted to the ground by thoughts of past failure or future uncertainty. In Hebrews 12:2 the writer speaks of those *who all their lives were held in slavery by their fear*. For some it may be the fear of possible rejection by family or friends, or of not making the grade or attaining the standard expected of them. With others, theirs is the fear of the past catching up with them and guilty secrets being exposed, or the fear which comes from doubting whether God could ever accept and use someone as frail or unworthy as they. Whatever the explanation or cause, fear can have a dreadfully debilitating effect and quickly reduce that person to being a spiritual and emotional wreck.

How urgently, therefore, we all need to learn the importance of trusting God in everything and appreciating that he has sent his very own Son to share each experience of life with us. Faith is not a matter of leaping blindly into the dark as some have suggested, any more than abseiling is wisely undertaken without instruction and careful preparation. Faith means examining the precious promises of God and taking hold of them. It demands all our attention—listening to what God is saying and carrying out his instructions to the letter. Above all, it involves recognising that Christ is there alongside of us, and appreciating the importance of maintaining regular communication with him. Take your eyes off him for a moment, and the waves which threatened to engulf Peter who but a few moments earlier had miraculously been walking upon them, will quickly begin to overwhelm us. Human fear has but one antidote—faith in the God who speaks and reveals his love in the person of his Son whom he has sent to be our Saviour and constant Friend.

4
Navigation

'Show me your ways, O Lord, teach me your paths;
guide me in your truth and teach me.'
(Psalm 25:4,5)

Sound navigation—the essence of safe movement in mountains. This was the cardinal rule we impressed upon all those who attended mountain activity courses at the Christian Mountain Centre. When visibility is obscured, whether by cloud, falling snow or even darkness, knowing exactly where you are and the direction you need to take will do much to allay anxiety and ensure a safe return.

There is a trend today in popular tourist areas to build cairns, daub rocks with coloured paint and even erect signposts to guide the visitor. Unfortunately this not only disfigures the natural landscape and turns the wilderness into little more than a nature-trail, but it also gives to travellers a false sense of security. If they believe their route to be clearly marked, people will have little awareness of any risk they are taking, even though they carry no map or compass, nor possess the skill to use them properly even if they had them with them. All they need do, or so they imagine, is follow the blobs of red paint or spot the next heap of stones. But paint quickly fades and cairns soon disappear under a sprinkling of snow. Paths are subject to erosion and rapidly become indistinct, while darkness, should the walker be overtaken by nightfall, will obliterate even the very best system of way-marking yet devised. No, there is absolutely no substitute for cultivating good navigational skills. Not even the very latest in GPS[1] electronic navigational equipment, which is now on offer (at a price!) to hill walkers, should ever be considered a replacement for the traditional means of route-finding by map and compass.

Derrick and I set off from Tanygrisiau, a village closely associated with the once thriving quarry industry of Cwmorthin, Rhosydd and Croesor, to walk to Llanfrothen within a mile or so of Derrick's home in Penrhyndeudraeth. We could have used one of two passes to cross the mountain-chain of Foel Ddu, Moel-yr-hydd, Moelwyn Mawr and Moelwyn Bach, but we were in the mood to claim some 'high ground', so we decided to take in the summit of Moelwyn Bach (2,346ft).

Derrick is my pastor. He came to our church some while after I was called to minister in Essex. Now that we have returned to Wales people sometimes ask how I get on with the person who is now doing my old 'job'. A strange question to my mind, but one to which I reply unhesitatingly 'Very well indeed.' We are of one mind concerning so many things. We share many interests (not least a love of the hills), and have the same burden for our neighbourhood, all of which has some bearing on the episode I will now narrate. When two people have much in common they love to talk. And talk we certainly did! We talked as we walked up the old quarry road toward Llyn Stwlan. We continued talking (albeit a little more breathlessly) as we scrambled up the steep hillside beneath Moel-yr-hydd. And we were still deep in conversation when we reached Bwlch Stwlan high above the lake and entered cloud. The weather certainly wasn't unpleasant by any means, but the cloud base was about nineteen hundred feet and soon visibility was no more than twenty-five metres.

There are numerous sheep-tracks on the Moelwyn but few recognisable paths. Not that this posed any real problem. We were making for the summit, so

---

[1]   Global Positioning System, makes use of 21 American military satellites orbiting the earth at a height of 12,400 miles and enables a person to pinpoint their position on land or sea to within 30-100 metres.

we just kept climbing until there was nothing more to climb. The circuitous route by which we approached the top hardly seemed to matter. We were, after all, conversing together and, with no views to take in on this occasion, were simply enjoying each other's company. We ate our muesli-bars and shared a flask of coffee by the summit cairn and after a brief rest prepared to descend. It was at this point we were to have our one and only significant disagreement of the day. We set off in exactly opposite directions! Of course we had every intention of walking together down the long spur westwards towards Llanfrothen. But which way was west? Each of us thought we knew, but clearly we couldn't both be right. Experience gained after many years in the hills gave one an instinctive 'feel' or sense of direction in such situations, I told myself. It was almost as if one had a 'natural' compass implanted in the brain telling you which was the correct way to go. The problem was Derrick's sense of direction and mine were not in agreement! It was obviously time to rummage in my rucksack and take out a proper compass. The initial reading suggested that Derrick was right and that I was wrong, but still I wasn't persuaded. I felt so sure that Llanfrothen and the sea lay in the opposite direction that I even searched my person for some metallic object that might be causing the compass needle to give an incorrect reading.

This just goes to show how strongly we feel that we are right on occasions, and equally how reluctant to accept that we may be wrong. It also underlines the rule we always taught our students at the Mountain Centre—always trust your compass, not your instinct! Once we were agreed which way was west and harmony had been restored, we set about planning a safe route off the summit. Light-hearted rivalry and 'leg-pulling' apart, this is no place in which to make a serious navigational error. Beyond the small summit plateau steep cliffs fall away on three sides of Moelwyn Bach. By carefully taking bearings from the map, however, we safely avoided dangerously steep ground and were soon emerging from the cloud on the crest of a broad grassy ridge with Llanfrothen directly ahead.

The route to Moelwyn Bach

The subject of guidance—knowing what God wants you to do—has always presented Christian believers with something of a challenge. It is one thing to believe that God has a plan for your life; it is another matter altogether to determine what the next step in that plan is and so translate it into real-life experience. That God has provided his people with the means by which they can discover the pathway he has prepared for them and so follow it, is beyond reasonable doubt. The principles or basic rules by which guidance may be obtained have been widely written about. That such principles are frequently neglected today, however, is also beyond dispute. In an age when it is far more fashionable to act purely on 'feelings' and embark on some venture declaring only that 'God has told me to do such and such', it would seem that a rediscovery of what the Bible says about guidance is long overdue.

It is essential, first of all, that we identify and possess the right tools for the job. I once met a man with a very frightened family perched precariously astride Crib Goch—a quite serious and extremely exposed knife-edge ridge which forms part of the Snowdon horseshoe. He wanted to know whether they were on the Pyg track, which was half a mile away and nearly a thousand feet lower down the mountain. I asked him if he possessed a map and he pulled from his pocket a tattered small scale Esso road map. It did have Snowdon marked—by a single black dot and a spot height which happened to be wrong! Here was a man ill-equipped for finding his way in the hills. In marked contrast God has given us two invaluable aids to guide us in the way he would have us go: his Word, the Bible, which we must carefully and regularly study, and his very own Holy Spirit to live within us. God's Spirit can interpret and apply God's Word and speak to us personally in the stillness of our own hearts. *Your word is a lamp to my feet and a light for my path*, said the psalmist (Psalm 119:105), whilst Jesus promised his disciples, *When he, the Spirit of truth, comes* (a promise fulfilled soon after his return to heaven), *he will guide you into all truth* (John 16:13). David's prayer in Psalm 143:10 is one we all need to pray: *Teach me to do your will, for you are my God; may your good Spirit lead me on level ground.* Remember also that God has provided us with Christian friends and church leaders to pray with us and wisely check out what we believe he is telling us to do. God has equipped us with his 'map and compass'. These, and only these, are reliable tools for the task in hand.

Once we have identified the tools God has provided, then we must learn to use them properly. I may claim to receive my guidance from the Bible, but if that means allowing it to fall open at random so that I can stick a pin in a verse with my eyes shut, I will never discover what God requires of me. Similarly, where the Holy Spirit is concerned, any activity (though allegedly attributed to him) which short-circuits or by-passes the mind in order to discover supernatural knowledge, should be viewed with grave misgiving. When church leaders in Jerusalem testified *It seemed good to the Holy Spirit and to us . . .* (Acts 15:28), it is clear that God had been at work granting wisdom to godly men who used their heads. Paul's advice to Timothy on this subject was *do your best [or study] to present yourself to God as one approved, a workman who does not need to be ashamed and who correctly handles the word of truth* (2 Timothy 2:15). Later he reminded Timothy that *from infancy* he had known *the holy Scriptures, which are able to make you wise . . . All Scripture is God-breathed and is useful for teaching, rebuking, correcting and training in righteousness, so that the man of God may be thoroughly equipped for every good work* (2 Timothy 3:15-17). God has provided all that we need in order to know his will and walk in his ways. We must learn to use that which he has given to us, in a spiritual and effective way.

If God has made such provision to guide us in life's pathway, and we have learned to use the means he has placed at our disposal, then we should trust him. My reluctance to trust my compass on Moelwyn Bach is not something of which I am proud. My senses are fallible. A good compass and an accurate map are not. They are trustworthy. To doubt that which is reliable, therefore, and instead allow yourself to be led by some ill-proven 'sixth sense' is stupid, to say the least. In spiritual terms Proverbs 3:5,6 says it all: *Trust in the Lord with all your heart and lean not on your own understanding; in all your ways acknowledge him, and he will direct your paths.*

Roman steps, Cwm Bychan

5
Ancient
Pathways

'Ask for the ancient paths.' (Jeremiah 6:16)

After a steady climb of about a mile up a grassy track we crested a ridge at a point 610 metres above sea level; just a few inches above two thousand feet—and we were riding bicycles! I have to confess that mountain biking has never been my favourite way to travel in the hills. The vast majority of mountain paths are far better suited to feet than wheels, whilst the erosion caused by knobbly-tyred machines skidding downhill can be considerable. Some tracks, however, are still classified as bridleways, and on this occasion I had good reason to ride rather than walk.

A friend of many years from Manchester was visiting—a superfit individual who would jog several miles each day carrying a rucksack full of books! His mountain fitness put me to shame, so when he suggested a walk in the hills my heart understandably sank. 'Have you ever tried mountain biking?' I asked. He replied that he hadn't. 'Good!' I responded, 'There's a spare machine in the shed—you can ride that.' My thinking was unashamedly selfish. I reasoned that as a relative 'newcomer' to the sport, his inexperience would hopefully compensate for my inferior stamina! I guess it did.

I had first cycled the 'green road' from Dyffryn Ardudwy to Pont Scethin

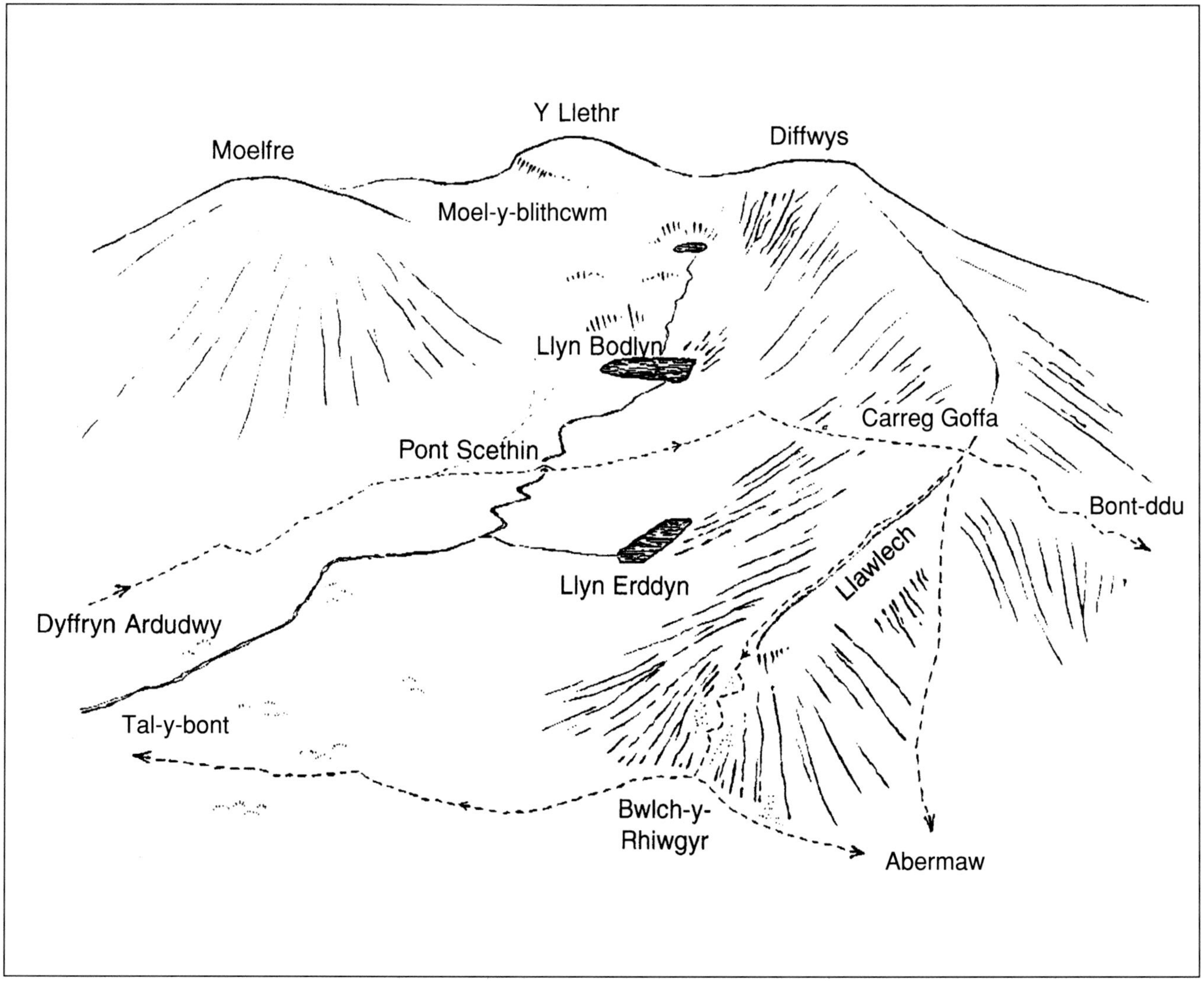

Area surrounding Pont Scethin

Moelfre

Y Llethr

Diffwys

Moel-y-blithcwm

Llyn Bodlyn

Carreg Goffa

Bont-ddu

Llawlech

Abermaw

Pont Scethin

Llyn Erddyn

Bwlch-y-Rhiwgyr

Dyffryn Ardudwy

Tal-y-bont

many years before. So indistinct is it in places that without a map it is quite difficult to follow. Indeed, when Pont Scethin is reached it is hard to understand why such an attractive and well-constructed bridge was ever built in such a marshy and remote place. Yet this ancient pathway was once the main coach road from Harlech to London—the M54/M6/M1 of the eighteenth century! The two of us rested on the bridge trying to imagine the stage-coach as it sped(?) with its passengers toward Dolgellau and beyond. What a journey!

To the south-east of Pont Scethin the route appears blocked by a lofty ridge running between Diffwys (2461ft.) in the east and Barmouth on the Cardigan Bay coast to the south. The path is still there, however, and with frequent pauses to consult the map we partly walked, partly rode diagonally up the steep hillside. Mid-way we came upon a grey-slate memorial stone erected by Melvyn Haigh, sometime Bishop of Winchester, in memory of his mother Janet who died in 1953. The tablet records that *Even as late as her eighty-fourth year, despite dim sight and stiffened joints she still loved to walk this way from Talybont to Penmaenpool.* What a remarkable character!

Urged on by her example and wondering how far we would be able to walk if we ever attained her grand age, we reached the crest of the ridge. The old coach road dropped down from this point to Bontddu on the Mawddach estuary, but we turned right to follow the ridge itself in a south-westerly direction—a glorious switchback ridden at speed along a grass track close-cropped over the years by countless sheep. Eventually a bone-jarring descent over boulders and loose scree brought us to Bwlch y Rhiwgyr—the second significant crossing point of this chain of hills. The path that crosses the ridge by this pass predated the coach road to the north-east by many centuries. It was the route preferred by the drovers taking their cattle from Anglesey and the Lleyn peninsular into England. It is reported that three thousand head of cattle passed this way annually in the seventeenth century, rising to a total in excess of ten thousand by the end of the eighteenth. But this particular path was well used long before it echoed to the cries of the drovers. As we adopted the undignified pose of

Memorial stone

downhill ski racers (or so we imagined) and speedily freewheeled back to Dyffryn Ardudwy on the coast, we passed numerous stone circles, cairns and, most impressive of all, a burial chamber known locally as Arthur's Quoit. The huge capstone was solid enough, but when Arthurian legend has been removed, relatively little is known about these tribes of prehistory who landed near Llanbedr from Spain and Brittany, and then gradually made their way inland. These were the builders of Megalithic cairns and cromlechs, whose paths were marked by *maen hir* or long stones, also called *maen gobaith* (guide stones, literally 'stones of hope') or *maen terfyn* (boundary stones), and who trod these hills even before the time of Abraham and the patriarchs.

Our ride had been completed comfortably in an afternoon, yet the route we followed encompassed more than three thousand years of history!

My interest in these ancient pathways set me thinking about the words found in Jeremiah 6:16. *This is what the Lord says: Stand at the crossroads and look; ask for the ancient paths, ask where the good way is, and walk in it, and you will find rest for your souls. But you said, 'We will not walk in it.'*

The paths walked by Megalithic tribespeople, marked by standing stones and cromlechs; the long-distance road from Caerhun in the Conwy valley to Carmarthen in the south, built by the Romans and known as Sarn Helen; the routes taken by stage-coach and cattle-drover—these are all paths of great antiquity. Few, if any, serve any useful purpose today. Sheep and the occasional hill-walker may still sometimes pass by, but of the identity and times of those early route-planners neither is likely to have any knowledge at all. Yet in their day these were paths of crucial importance. They assisted migration, linked communities, promoted trade and enabled armies to move speedily from place to place. Of course, times have now changed and modern forms of transport require a modern road and rail network, with the result that the ancient paths inevitably lie unused and largely forgotten. Yet Jeremiah's call should set alarm-bells ringing in other realms. In an age when scientific frontiers are being pushed further and further back, and the human mind claims to be more and more liberated and open to new ideas, Bible truth and God-given ways are in danger of becoming ever more eroded. There are those who believe Christian doctrine needs to be made more palatable and Christian worship more appealing to our 'rock and roll' orientated society. A new spirit of tolerance toward, and co-operation with, other faiths is called for. We are led to believe that Christian religion must move with the times.

Jeremiah's appeal is not for a return to an outdated form of religion incomprehensible to modern man. His argument is that, where God is concerned, the truths we are to believe about him and the way we are to behave before him are firmly established and cannot change. There are specific principles by which our lives are to be ordered. There are particular truths clearly set out in the Bible which may be unpopular with many but which we must cling to and contend for.

We might think, for example, of Hebrews 11 with its long list of men and women who trod the time-tested pathway of *faith*. Here were people who gained great wisdom, strength and courage by believing not only that God is real, but that he was with them and at work in their lives. Their righteousness before God was not earned by personal effort or religious zeal, but received as a free and gracious gift by faith. Only by following in their footsteps, as we are urged to do in Hebrews 12:1-3, will we ourselves discover the secret of their remarkable testimony.

Another 'ancient pathway' described in God's Word which I long to know better in my own Christian walk is the pathway of *holiness*. The prophet Isaiah saw this pathway very clearly. *And a highway will be there; it will be called the Way of Holiness. The unclean will not journey on it; it will be for those who walk in that Way; wicked fools will not go about on it . . . only the redeemed will walk there, and the ransomed of the Lord will return. They will enter Zion with singing; everlasting joy will crown their heads* (Isaiah 35:8-10). In a day of lowered standards, when the difference between right and wrong is so blurred that morality has become little more than the way a person 'feels', we need to realise that God's standards have not changed and that his requirements of righteousness, truth and justice are still relevant and will be the basis upon which all will finally be judged.

I can't help thinking of the great need today in Christian circles for a rediscovery of and return to the 'dual carriageway' of *sacrifice* and *service*. How often do certain preachers tell us that it is a relatively easy thing for a person to become a Christian, and that the Christian life is an exciting adventure from start to finish! Jesus didn't say this. He warned that the track to be taken would be hard to find, difficult to follow and ignored by all but a few (Matthew 7:13,14). He spoke in terms of self-denial and personal sacrifice. *If anyone would come after me*, he said, *he must deny himself and take up his cross and follow me. For whoever wants to save his life will lose it, but whoever loses his life for me and for the gospel will save it. What good is it for a man to gain the whole world, yet forfeit his soul? Or what can a man give in exchange for his soul?* (Mark 8:34-37). In Romans 12:1,2 Paul urged his readers, in view of God's mercy toward them, to offer their bodies as living sacrifices, holy and pleasing to God. Belonging to a generation that has tended to popularise (even glamorise) Christian discipleship and present it as a 'fun-thing', we need to recognise that there is a cost involved. Self-will and ambition need to be surrendered. I must adopt the attitude of Christ in Gethsemane—*Nevertheless not my will, but yours, be done*, and conform not to the world, but to all that is good, acceptable and pleasing to God (Romans 12:2).

There are other pathways the Bible urges us to seek out and follow. The three I have briefly described are the most important and these I long to explore more fully. They are *ancient* pathways, but that is not to be held against them. Indeed, their very antiquity shows that they have stood the test of time and proved reliable for succeeding generations.

The path of the righteous is like the first gleam of dawn, shining ever brighter till the full light of day. But the way of the wicked is like deep darkness; they do not know what makes them stumble (Proverbs 4:18,19).

Join me in your imagination as we stand in the steep-sided valley which contains the two-mile-long Llyn Cowlyd reservoir midway between Dolgarrog and Capel Curig. This is a wild and remote place. Lose your way up here and you are surrounded by one hundred square miles of inhospitable terrain without a single dwelling or road to lead you to safety. From the north-west shore of the lake a mountainside of scree and crag rears up steeply one thousand four hundred feet to the summit of the aptly named Pen Llithrig y Wrach (literally: the slippery head of the witch), two thousand six hundred feet above sea level. On the far side of the lake the ground rises in similar fashion to the top of Creigiau Gleision. These mountains do not attract tourists, so visitors are few. We stand alone with only sheep and the occasional buzzard mewing overhead for company. Yet the path we are on is part of Sarn Helen, where on the wind, it is claimed, one can still hear the distant sound of Roman legions on the march. By this route eighteen hundred years ago messengers travelled, pack-mules moved vital supplies, and troops were deployed to quell unrest and enforce law and order. This is an ancient pathway of which the vast majority of motorists speeding up the A5 are totally unaware.

May God never permit his paths to suffer such neglect or allow a time to come when we are so ignorant of his ways.

From Snowdon summit

6
Cloud

'A voice out of the cloud.' (Mark 9:1-18)

We stood on the summit, our crampons biting reassuringly into the snow-ice beneath our feet. Overhead the sun shone from a clear blue sky. Below and to the east as far as the eye could see stretched an ocean of white cloud. Here and there other peaks, breaking through, appeared to float like islands in a sea of cotton-wool. It was one of those January days you tend to dream about.

I had not met the other two prior to our encounter that day on the top of Snowdon, but sharing a sense of exhilaration and deep pleasure quickly removes that shyness and reserve for which we as a race are so well known. Soon we were eating lunch together and talking enthusiastically of our experiences of that morning. We had ascended the mountain by different routes; from opposite directions, in fact. I had set out from Rhyd-ddu to the south-west, sheltered from a biting east wind and enjoying bright sunshine all the way. When the top of my head began to burn (it has less natural cover now than it used to have!) I had resorted to tying knots in the corners of a handkerchief and wearing it as a hat for protection. In marked contrast, however, my two new friends had started from Pen-y-pass to the north-east, having debated whether or not it was really sensible to do so given the strong wind, freezing temperature and low cloud cover. The conditions that prevailed on their side of the mountain promised nothing but hard work and considerable discomfort; perhaps even risk.

Maybe it was the total *unexpectedness* of this sudden transition that made their 'mountain-top' joy even greater than mine. From cold, damp cloud which had restricted their visibility to all but a few yards, they had entered a world of brilliant sunshine and clear blue sky in almost as little time as it takes to tell. After all, I'd had some idea of what was in store from the moment I set out, and had been anticipating that pleasure for some two hours or more. For them it was the very last thing they expected, and for that reason was surely all the more satisfying.

That two such contrasting 'worlds' could both exist at one and the same time and in the same vicinity may be hard to accept, but we know it can happen. And this can help us to appreciate an even greater mystery. In three of the Gospels' records we read of two markedly different scenes; one in the valley where darkness and despair reigned, and the other on a nearby mountain top where dazzling brightness and divine glory were displayed. Furthermore, both of these occurred simultaneously. Matthew 17:1-18, Mark 9:1-18 and Luke 9:28-40 describe an occasion when Jesus, accompanied by Peter, James and John, ascended a mountain, leaving the other nine disciples on their own for a while. In their master's absence, these were confronted by a man whose son was possessed by an evil spirit. The father had undoubtedly heard of Christ's power to cast out evil spirits, but on their own the nine were apparently quite unable to help. Given their master's reputation it would have been assumed that they could have rendered some assistance. In the event they were powerless in this encounter with such a strong enemy. Gloom and despondency, like a thick cloud, enveloped the small company in the valley. But at precisely the same moment a very different scene was unfolding on the summit of the mountain. Jesus, in the presence of Peter, James and John, was being 'transfigured'—that is, his appearance was so changed that he shone with a brightness that eclipsed even the sun. The only adequate explanation for this is that for a brief moment the glorious splendour he had laid aside when he left heaven for earth was restored to him by God. The three privileged disciples were allowed to see Jesus in a totally new light. Years later John recalled the event when he wrote, *We have seen his glory, the glory of the one and only Son, who came from the Father* (John 1:14), whilst Peter spoke of their having been *eyewitnesses of his majesty* (2 Peter 1:16). In addition to this glimpse of Christ's heavenly splendour, the disciples were also allowed to witness a meeting which took place when Moses and Elijah appeared and talked with Jesus about his imminent death. From Peter's reaction it is difficult to know precisely what the disciples made of this at the time, but given the importance of these two men in Old Testament history, it is surely possible to see in this something of Christ's even greater role in God's eternal plan of salvation. Finally, a cloud momentarily obscured from view the departure of Moses and Elijah, and from the cloud the voice of God himself was heard to speak—*This is my Son, whom I love. Listen to him!* All in all, a remarkable testimony to the uniqueness of the Lord Jesus Christ—testimony to the *splendour* he had temporarily set aside; to his *supremacy* over even the greatest men of sacred history, and to his divine *Sonship*.

When we are struggling in the valley, defeated and downcast, with no clear understanding of what is happening because of the thick cloud all around us, it is then that we especially need to appreciate all that the three disciples saw and heard on the mountain top. In the valley the nine disciples presumably blamed their failure on the fact that Christ was absent. Mary, in John 11:32, did the same thing: *Lord, if you had been here, my brother would not have died.* How easy it is to assume that because Christ cannot be seen in a particular situation, his influence and power must be severely limited. Yet all the while, hidden from human gaze, he is clothed with majesty and reigns in power—power which he is ready and willing to employ in the interest of those who acknowledge his lordship and seek his help. The centurion in Luke 7:7 exhibited such faith. Though undeserving of having Christ enter his home, he nevertheless sent this message: *Say the word, and my servant will be healed.* In this life, 'valley' experiences will be commonplace. Jesus promised that *in this world you will have trouble* (John 16:33). But he also claimed victory over the world—victory he shares with his people.

The Snowdon Range

Lunch finished, it was time to descend. Before we left the summit we stood for a few more moments on the very edge of Clogwyn y Garnedd, the steep cliff that falls away to the north-east. Somewhere beneath that white ocean of cloud lay Llyn Glaslyn and Cwm Dyli. The sun on our backs cast a shadow of the mountain on the cloud below, complete with the clearly discernible outline of three human figures. Like children we waved and the shadows waved back. But even more striking, each of the shadowy figures had its own halo of bright light encircling the head! The Brocken Spectre, as it is called, is not uncommon in high mountains, but because it requires the sun above and cloud beneath, it is a rare occurrence in these islands. There is, of course, a physical explanation for this phenomenon. It is neither an omen of impending disaster, as some have thought, nor a sign of personal sanctity (even though each observer can only see his or her own halo)! And yet, as the sun shining in its strength thus imparts just a little of its splendour to each shadow, so Christ delights to bestow his grace upon those who are prepared to acknowledge, obey and trust in him. Some time in the future the Christian believer will dwell in everlasting light and gaze constantly upon the glory of Christ. Until that day dawns we live in a frequently hostile environment. Rain, wind and fog will all be encountered. Storm clouds will threaten. But out of the cloud the true believer will hear a voice speak—*This is my Son, whom I love. Listen to him!*

Elsa

7
Elsa

'The Son of Man came to seek and to save what was lost.'
(Luke 15:4-7; 19:10)

Elsa was a very special member of our household. Though devoted to our children and perfectly trustworthy with the young people who stayed at the Christian Mountain Centre, she was not primarily a family pet. She came to us for one reason and one reason only—to be trained and used for search and rescue in the mountains. Toward the end of her working life she was joined by Khola who, like her, was also a German shepherd. ('Khola' was Nepalese for 'little stream'; aptly named as a puppy!) He was great fun to work with, but the 'retirement' of his handler from active search and rescue work denied him the opportunity of ever equalling Elsa's success in this field.

We had Elsa from a puppy and she lived for eight years. She came from a breeder who regularly supplied the police. Though considered too small for police training, her lighter than average weight made her remarkably agile and swift over rough terrain. She was a mountain dog through and through. Winter training, which included practice in avalanche search techniques, took place in Glencoe annually, when each dog's agility was assessed on the notorious Aonach Eagach ridge. This is an exposed and extremely hazardous route under winter conditions, even for experienced and well-equipped climbers, but one none the less on which Elsa always seemed perfectly at ease. On several occasions, having grown tired of waiting at the foot of the cliff on which I was

teaching rock climbing, she would suddenly 'appear' on the ledge where I was belayed and sit by my side! This was something we clearly had to discourage, particularly on harder climbs, but it was discouragement Elsa never really understood.

Before the formation of the Welsh Unit of the Search and Rescue Dog Association, all searches for people missing in the hills were undertaken by volunteers on foot, supported where appropriate by helicopters of 'C' Flight, 22 Squadron, RAF Valley. This necessarily limited operations to the hours of daylight, which on occasions resulted in a casualty dying from exposure during the night before a thorough search could be organised. However, it had already been shown in the Alps and in Scotland that a trained dog could cover the same area that would normally require at least ten men to search properly—more if the ground was at all broken. Furthermore, because a dog worked on the basis of airborne scent rather than sight, it could operate just as well at night and even locate a victim buried under several feet of snow. Even so, the police who were responsible for coordinating any search in the hills of North Wales were initially sceptical, and the dogs that were being trained had to prove themselves in a dramatic way before they were taken at all seriously and accorded their rightful place in the Mountain Rescue service. One such exploit was credited to Elsa.

Quite early on in her training, Elsa had been introduced to the idea of searching for victims buried in the snow. One January our eldest son's primary school teacher called us in to discuss what she considered to be 'the problem of Mark's over-fertile imagination.' Apparently, the children in her class had been asked to draw a picture of something that had occurred during the Christmas holidays. Our son's picture showed 'daddy burying mummy in the snow'; something, Mark told his teacher, his father had done most days during the holidays! 'Yes, that's quite correct,' I told a clearly surprised teacher, 'but didn't he draw or at least tell you about the dog we are training?' He hadn't, of course, so lengthy explanation was needed to convince the dear lady that she wasn't dealing with the most eccentric family on the face of the earth!

One Saturday, however, it was no longer a case of a puppy playing a game of 'hide and seek' in the snow. During the afternoon a group of soldiers had become totally disorientated in 'whiteout' conditions high above Cwm Glas on Snowdon. A whiteout occurs when thick cloud and falling snow merge with snow already lying on the ground, to make not only route-finding but even maintaining one's balance extremely difficult. Realising they were lost, the lieutenant in charge went to reconnoitre. When he did not return after two hours the company found their own way down the mountain to raise the alarm. As daylight faded an RAF rescue team already on the mountain carried out a quick search of the most likely places where an accident might have occurred, including a descent of Parsley Fern gully. They found nothing and withdrew to await first light next day.

At about the time that the RAF team came off the mountain my telephone rang. The police were requesting that dogs be taken into the search area. Thankfully it had stopped snowing and the cloud had lifted as three handlers with their dogs began systematically to contour the steep slopes of Cwm Uchaf and Cwm Glas. It was some time after midnight that I reached Parsley Fern gully, wanting Elsa to continue into the far side of the cwm. I could see the footprints in the gully left by the RAF team the previous afternoon, and was somewhat annoyed that Elsa seemed more interested in the tracks they had left, than searching the fresh terrain beyond. Higher and higher up the gully she went, ignoring my calls. Then she stopped and started digging in the snow, occasionally barking. She had removed about 50 cms of snow by the time I reached her, and in the circle of light from my headtorch I saw the body of a young man. Would that I could report he was only injured and made a full recovery. Sadly he had died instantly in a fall of several hundred feet and had been buried under a mass of snow that had followed him down the gully. The RAF team had actually scrambled over the avalanche debris, with no way of knowing he was there.

Tragic though the outcome was, Elsa had demonstrated just how successfully dogs could operate in this kind of situation. The Dog Unit would have further successes in the years to follow, some with far happier endings than this one. I have to confess that on a number of occasions when woken by the telephone at one o'clock in the morning, I would far sooner have turned over and gone back to sleep. But such reluctance on the part of the handler was never observed in the dog. Whenever the harness she wore for 'work' was produced, there was at once an alertness and excitement shown by Elsa that we saw at no other time. Day or night she was ready to do whatever was required of her.

We see such commitment and dedication displayed by a shepherd in Luke 15:4-7. Jesus spoke of a man who was unfortunate enough to lose one of the hundred sheep he owned. To lose just one out of a hundred might not be considered all that serious. In today's business world, a mere 1% loss through damage or theft would be deemed quite acceptable. But that was not how the shepherd in the story saw things. Such high value did he place on the one missing sheep, that he was prepared to *leave the ninety-nine in the wilderness* (perhaps exposing all of them to some danger in shepherding terms) while he went in search of the one that was lost. Clearly the untiring efforts and selfless perseverance of this man were intended to show the immeasurable value God places on just one human being, and illustrate the lengths to which Christ was prepared to go in his determination *to seek and to save what was lost.*

This resolve and dedication appear in the **price** Jesus was prepared to pay. If the shepherd in the story was ready and willing to leave the ninety-nine other sheep with all the risk that involved, how much more was Christ prepared to leave in His desire to reach and rescue lost sinners! He *made himself nothing, taking the very nature of a servant, being made in human likeness. And being found in appearance as a man, he humbled himself and became obedient to death—even death on a cross!* (Philippians 2:7,8). What sacrifice, and all for sinners, every single one of whom was uniquely precious to him.

We see it also in his **endurance.** When lesser individuals would surely have been tempted to call off the search for the sheep, the shepherd in Luke 15:4

carries on *until he finds it*. How much like Jesus who, even when his own followers sought to hold him back, nevertheless *stedfastly set his face to go to Jerusalem* (Luke 9:51 AV). Only by dying for them on the cross could the salvation of each of his sheep be secured. Therefore he allowed nothing to stand in his way, but *for the joy set before him endured the cross, scorning its shame* and consequently has now *sat down at the right hand of the throne of God* (Hebrews 12:2). Finally, Christ's great desire and determination to save those who are in darkness and danger is seen in the **joy** which accompanied the successful conclusion of his mission. The shepherd joyfully returned with the missing animal and called his friends and neighbours together to celebrate the recovery of that which meant so much to him—an act of rejoicing echoing the praise heard in heaven whenever a single sinner repents and is recovered by Christ. Would that each reader might know true forgiveness, joy and peace in the warm embrace of the Seeker and Saviour of the lost!

8
Rescue

'He . . . brought me up out of a horrible pit . . . and set my feet upon a rock.'
(Psalm 40:1-3)

There have been several occasions in the mountains when I have had reason to marvel at God's timing, overruling or intervention, but none more so than the one I shall now describe. If there was ever a time when God acted in a quite remarkable way in the interest of someone seriously injured in a mountain accident, this was it—a fact that did not go unnoticed by other rescue team members who, in the normal course of events, would not have given God credit for anything.

It was a typical mountain day—wet, windy and with low cloud reducing visibility to twenty metres. Hardly a fitting reward for anyone who had just walked to the top of Snowdon, some might say. But our spirits were not dampened. The young people in my charge on a course at the Christian Mountain Centre had already come to accept that these were precisely the conditions needed in which to try out the basic skills of safe movement and sound navigation they were being taught. Before the end of the day, however, we were all to learn lessons that went far beyond those set out in the course syllabus!

It all began when, without any warning, a window-like opening appeared in the cloud, giving us a narrow but nevertheless clear view across the cwm to the summit ridge of Crib y Ddysgl. It was the only time the heavy curtain of cloud

61

Area of the rescue

was to part, and the gap that appeared lasted for less than a minute. Yet in those brief moments before that small section of distant ridge was again obscured, we witnessed a man stumble and fall. Whether he had companions with him who were sufficiently experienced to deal with the situation, and how far he had fallen or how badly he was hurt, we had no way of knowing. But we had seen enough and at once set off across Bwlch Glas to see what we could do to help.

Twelve minutes later we reached them—a small group of very frightened schoolchildren who had seen their teacher slip on wet rock and disappear from view down the broken cliff known as Garnedd Ugain. Fortunately he had not fallen far and was still conscious when we reached him, but he had sustained some very severe facial injuries and clearly needed to be evacuated swiftly and taken to hospital before his condition deteriorated further. People have died in the hills from the effects of shock and hypothermia when their injuries were not so severe, simply because it took so long to locate them and get them off the mountain. We were well aware of this, as were two experienced hill-walkers who had joined us. They immediately set off for Pen y Pass to summon help. We calculated it would be three hours at least before a rescue team equipped with a stretcher would reach the scene of the accident, plus a further two-hour carry to get the injured man to an ambulance for the journey to hospital. And five hours is a long time for someone suffering such distress and pain. The seriousness of the situation was felt by all, as we tended to his injuries and, together with much silent prayer, did what we could to make him as comfortable as possible.

Some readers may be wondering at this point about the use of radios and those yellow helicopters so frequently seen buzzing around the hills of Snowdonia. The answer is simple. No helicopter can operate safely in dense cloud, so evacuation by air seemed out of the question. Furthermore, whilst I did indeed carry a radio tuned to the Mountain Rescue (M/R) frequency, I also needed someone to switch on and operate the powerful base-set located at the rescue post before I could speak to anyone, and until news of our emergency reached them, this would not be done.

So why, it might be asked, did I risk running down my radio batteries by repeatedly transmitting a call for assistance when nobody was supposed to be listening? Why indeed! But even more inexplicably, why did a Search and Rescue helicopter from 22 Squadron, RAF Valley, flying above the cloud, have its radio switched to the M/R channel, when it would normally be expected to be using the more common Air Traffic Control frequency? It would seem that whilst returning from a rescue mission in mid-Wales, they had simply delayed switching channels! Result? I was speaking in person to the navigator of a rescue helicopter flying directly overhead. By now we could hear the throbbing of the engine, and it was this fact that led the crew to make a bold decision. Because the injured man lay but thirty feet below the highest point on the ridge, the pilot requested us to talk him down through the cloud cover. As long as we could hear the aircraft above us, there was little risk of it hitting the hillside. Slowly and with ever-increasing noise it emerged from the cloud and hovered immediately above our heads. The winchman lowered not only a stretcher but also a doctor who had been on board. Soon the casualty was being hoisted back into the aircraft and, within little more than an hour after he slipped and fell, the schoolteacher was admitted to Ysbyty Gwynedd Accident Unit at Bangor.

Following plastic surgery the man made a full recovery and wrote me a letter in which he praised a rescue service which had but to 'switch on a radio set and summons a helicopter, all in the space of a few minutes'! Of course, I wrote back and told him the truth—namely, that we firmly believed God had intervened, not once but a number of times in a quite remarkable way, to bring about a far from 'normal' deliverance.

Whilst this story has taken longer to recount than others in this book, it is told because it illustrates so clearly God's merciful and gracious dealings with weak and frail people who so easily make mistakes and so frequently fall into sin. Even the most upright and godly of men and women whose lives are described in the Bible are shown to be capable of serious error and sin. They may well have seen much of God's glory and enjoyed close fellowship with him, and because of this they may have achieved great things for him. Their faith may be reported in such a way as to challenge and inspire similar devotion in us. But for all that, they were still sinners who frequently had to weep over their failure to live as God had demanded, and who were ever mindful of their complete dependence upon his mercy. The writer of Psalm 130, aware of this, wrote, *Out of the depths I cry to you, O Lord; O Lord, hear my voice. Let your ears be attentive to my cry for mercy. If you, O Lord, kept a record of sins, O Lord, who could stand?* (verses 1-3).

Such a statement could come only from one who was both fully aware of the depths into which his sinful nature had led him, and who at the same time recognised the absolute holiness of a God in whom no sin is found. He readily acknowledged the seriousness of his fall and the pain his actions had caused. He made no attempt to excuse himself or blame others for his mistakes. He, and he alone, was at fault. Yet, for all that, he did not sink deeper into despair, but rather cried from the depths to God. And what is the ground of his hope? *But with you there is forgiveness; therefore you are feared* (Psalm 130:4).

Psalm 130 may not be attributed to David, but David was certainly a man whose spiritual emotions at times scaled the heights of fellowship with God and at others plumbed the depths of disobedience and despair. It is hard to conceive that the author of Psalm 23, who is described in 1 Samuel 13:14 as *a man after God's own heart*, could fail God so miserably and commit the most heinous of sins. Yet even in the tearful outpouring of his heart in Psalm 51 we see the very same hope that burns in Psalm 130:4. *Have mercy on me, O God, according to your unfailing love; according to your great compassion blot out my transgressions. Wash away all my iniquity and cleanse me from my sin. For I know my transgressions, and my sin is always before me. Against you, you only, have I sinned and done what is evil in your sight, so that you are proved right when you speak and justified when you judge . . . Hide your face from my sins and blot out all my iniquity . . . Do not cast me from your presence or take your Holy Spirit from me. Restore to me the joy of your salvation . . .*

Then I will teach transgressors your ways, and sinners will turn back to you (Psalm 51:1-4,9,11-13).

Like David and all those who both preceded and followed him, we too will inevitably fall into sin and fail God. We deceive ourselves and call God a liar if we think otherwise (1 John 1:8,10). This being so, we need to recognise and avoid two common misapprehensions.

First of all, we should not underestimate the seriousness of any sin we may commit. In the church of Paul's day were some who felt that God's grace was so free and powerful, that it didn't really matter whether they sinned or not. His mercy somehow 'eclipsed' the awfulness of human sin. But it doesn't. And if we make excuses or forgive ourselves too readily when we succumb to temptation and fall into sin, then any cry to God for mercy will be suspect; indeed, we may never truly repent or seek his forgiveness at all. The man lying on a narrow ledge three thousand feet up a mountain, with his face smashed beyond recognition, did not need to be told that his plight was serious. His groaning said it all. Maybe there are times when we need to look long and hard at the way we are, and realise that if our sin was serious enough for Christ to suffer and die on the cross for it, then it is certainly serious enough to cause us pain and tears and grief even now.

But equally important, in the second place, we should never despair, thinking that our sin is so dreadful that it has somehow put us beyond the reach of God's mercy and that we now have no hope of ever being forgiven. Because our willingness to forgive our fellows will often depend upon the seriousness of the offence they have committed, or how frequently they may have hurt us, it is all too easy to imagine that God's forgiveness is dispensed in a similar way. Therefore, when we fail him especially badly or repeatedly fall into the same sin, it is very easy to believe (particularly with Satan telling us so) that we have gone just too far this time; that God's mercy has simply been exhausted as far as we are concerned. But God, thankfully, does not forgive as we so often forgive each other. God, in all his ways, is supernatural. And just as, in the episode I have related, God was pleased to act in a way that was far beyond our understanding and expectations, so in the realm of his compassion and grace it is his prerogative and delight to show mercy toward us again and again and again. The way he forgives, and his reasons for doing so, are as miraculous and beyond comprehension as any of his other activities in heaven or on earth.

That unforgettable day on Snowdon, we witnessed first hand God's ability to intervene and deliver someone who very literally had fallen from the pathway. No less wonderful is the spiritual truth illustrated by this story. David in Psalm 103 declared: *Praise the Lord, O my soul, and forget not all his benefits. He forgives all your sins and heals all your diseases; he redeems your life from the pit and crowns you with love and compassion . . . The Lord is compassionate and gracious, slow to anger, abounding in love. He will not always accuse, nor will he harbour his anger for ever; he does not treat us as our sins deserve or repay us according to our iniquities. For as high as the heavens are above the earth, so great is his love for those who fear him; as far as the east is from the west, so far has he removed our transgressions from us* (Psalm 103:2-4,8-12).

Ruined building in Rhosydd Slate Quarry

9
Dereliction

'Thorns will overrun her citadels, nettles and brambles her strongholds.'
(Isaiah 34:13)

Whilst the mountains hold many pleasures for the climber or hill-walker, and are capable of imparting moments of almost indescribable joy, there have been occasions when I have felt a degree of sadness and have come away from a particular area with something of a heavy heart.

It is not at all uncommon, when walking in our hills, to come across the ruined remains of once impressive buildings or even whole communities. Some may have been comparatively small hafodydd or farmsteads intended primarily for summer occupation, whereas others cover a huge area and represent a once thriving industry quarrying slate or mining copper. Strange though it may seem, it is not the disfigurement of the landscape caused by some of these larger enterprises that saddens me. Although large excavations or heaps of quarry waste do indeed represent human intrusion into the natural environment, there is a sense in which the passage of time has caused the man-made to 'blend' with its surroundings. The quite haphazard way in which buildings tumble and become a rich haven of mosses, lichens and ferns frequently gives them an attractiveness all their own. No, it is not the suggestion that such sites 'spoil' the landscape that makes me sad. I don't think they necessarily do. Rather it is the fact that at such locations one is confronted by a scene of widespread abandonment and decay.

With just a slight knowledge of local history, I close my eyes in these places and picture extensive human activity. Yes, there was dirt and danger that would be intolerable in today's world of trade unions and health and safety inspectors. There was also great social injustice as quarry-owners exploited their workforces inexcusably. But this was industrial life at the turn of the nineteenth century, when proud men were prepared to suffer great hardship in order to keep a roof over the heads of their family. As I write, one particular quarry keeps coming into my mind—the Rhosydd, midway between the mountain village of Coesor and Tanygrisiau near Blaenau Ffestiniog. Many times I have walked among the ruined buildings and have even ventured into the vast underground chambers from which high quality slate was blasted (exploration of which is now sadly forbidden for reasons of safety). The immense size of the caverns and the massive pieces of rusting machinery left behind when the quarry closed can only generate the deepest respect for those who worked there.

On one exploratory visit I picked up a cardboard box which appeared to have been discarded only the day before. It bore the insignia of the Nobel Explosives Company incorporating the signature of Alfred Nobel (later of 'peace prize' fame), and I thought of the danger those who handled such material were prepared to face in order to support their families—families from which some who came from further afield were necessarily separated from early on a Monday morning until Saturday afternoon, during which time they were accommodated in crowded barracks within the quarry itself, with only the stream from which to draw water. In 1899 nineteen quarries in the immediate vicinity of Blaenau Ffestiniog employed 3515 men and produced 112,733 tons of slate. Fifteen years later all of these figures were reduced by more than half, a four-day working week having been introduced in 1908. With the world-wide demand for slate dropping each year, the days of this mighty industry were numbered.

Today the Rhosydd lies abandoned, silent save for the cry of ravens and the occasional chough, a scene of dereliction and decay. The social changes which led to the closure of this huge quarry and others like it cannot be discussed in this short chapter. Nor can we contribute to the debate currently taking place as to whether or not the reopening of the Rhosydd and Cwmorthin quarry would be economically viable. For me these sites of neglect and ruin, these silent memorials to human achievement and endeavour, carry a far more solemn lesson.

The Bible frequently describes once great and powerful nations as reduced to heaps of rubble on account of unrighteousness and injustice. For example, because they refused to repent of their idolatry and seek mercy from God, Isaiah warned the Edomites of approaching ruin in these terms: *God will stretch out over Edom the measuring-line of chaos and the plumb line of desolation. Her nobles will have nothing there to be called a kingdom, all her princes will vanish away. Thorns will overrun her citadels, nettles and brambles her strongholds. She will become a haunt for jackals, a home for owls. Desert creatures will meet with hyenas, and wild goats will bleat to each other; there the night creatures will also repose and find themselves places of rest* (Isaiah 34:11b-14).

But it was not just the idolatrous nations of the Old Testament who needed to heed such solemn warnings. One has only to look at the large number of Welsh nonconformist chapels, many of them built around the turn of the last century in the aftermath of great spiritual blessing, which have either become carpet warehouses or snooker clubs, or else have crumbled into a state of total disrepair. Whatever happened to the large congregations that once filled their pews? Or what became of the powerful preaching that moved so many men and women to tears under the convicting influence of the Spirit of God?

Then again, what was responsible for such a tragic decline in the spiritual life of the Welsh nation can also spell ruin in the experience of individuals. How often has a young person shown great zeal for God and for God's service, only to have that enthusiasm diminish later on to the serious detriment of their Christian testimony? Whilst the causes for such spiritual decay will vary from one person

The Fron chapel, Penrhyndeudraeth

to another, the example of Demas in 2 Timothy 4:10 is fairly typical. With great sadness Paul reports the desertion of Demas because he loved this world.

Whether it was worldly philosophy that led to a decline in the spiritual life of the nation, or worldly pleasure that has wrecked the witness of a particular individual, it amounts to the same thing. When other things are permitted to replace the concerns of God in our lives, then the rot has already set in. John puts it quite bluntly: *Do not love the world or anything in the world. If anyone loves the world, the love of the Father is not in him. For everything in the world—the cravings of sinful man, the lust of his eyes and the boasting of what he has and does—comes not from the Father but from the world. The world and its desires pass away, but the man who does the will of God lives for ever* (1 John 2:15-17).

On a hill above the village of Penrhyndeudraeth stood an abandoned chapel building. Exposed to the elements and at the mercy of vandals, it was in danger of becoming derelict in only a short period of time. In the purposes of God this building without a congregation was brought to the attention of a company of Christians who were without a building in which to worship. No service had been held in Capel Fron for over ten years, but when the key was obtained and the building was inspected, a Bible was found on the pulpit opened at Jeremiah 29:10-14—*This is what the Lord says: . . . 'I will come to you and fulfil my gracious promise to bring you back to this place. For I know the plans I have for you,' declares the Lord, 'plans to prosper you and not to harm you, plans to give you hope and a future. Then you will call upon me and come and pray to me, and I will listen to you. You will seek me and find me when you seek me with all your heart. I will be found by you,' declares the Lord, 'and will bring you back from captivity.'*

Following its purchase, the building was refurbished and became a focal point of spiritual life and gospel preaching in the locality. It is also a testimony to all that God is able to do in the experience of a person whose spiritual life may be in an advanced state of deterioration and decay. When rot and rust are a constant threat, we need someone who specialises in rebirth and reconstruction. In the Lord Jesus Christ we have that someone.

10
Feed my Lambs

'He tends his flock like a shepherd:
He gathers the lambs in his arms and carries them close to his heart;
he gently leads those that have young.'
(Isaiah 40:11)

Looking back, some of my happiest moments in the hills have been spent not in the company of other experienced climbers undertaking a serious rock climb or expedition, but with children as they were introduced to mountains for the very first time in their lives.

Our own sons grew up surrounded by the hills and scrambled about on outcrops of rock behind our home in Beddgelert from a very early age. For a 'treat' on his sixth birthday Mark was given his first taste of real rock climbing. On summer afternoons the one-hundred-and-fifty-feet slab of Tryfan Bach in the Ogwen valley is swarming with novice rock climbers, but in April it was ours to enjoy alone as father and son roped up at the foot of the climb. At that age children show little fear of heights and climb with a natural ability that sadly forsakes most folk within a relatively few years. Following the lines of cracks up the otherwise smooth slab of rock Mark climbed easily. Belayed midway, he handled the rope with confidence, paying it out for me as I climbed on (taking great care as I did so not to test his ability to arrest the fall of a leader over four times his own weight!). Reaching the top of the climb his face was wreathed in a smile. It was the best birthday treat anyone could ever have, he told me. He had completed his very first real rock climb!

Twenty-six years later Mark and I returned to the Ogwen valley and ascended Tryfan by the always exciting north ridge. He now had two children of his own, and as we looked down on Tryfan Bach from high on the mountain, he recalled the day we climbed together and spoke of his intention to bring his own children to the place, that they might experience in turn the joy he had known so long before.

The Christian Mountain Centre was one of the very first outdoor pursuit centres in Snowdonia to arrange courses for children of pre-secondary school age. It was generally felt at that time that children below the age of fourteen would gain little from exposure to a mountain environment, and that in any case the risks involved were too great. Perhaps it was the fact that we had children of our own who had learned to climb and ski, and had developed good mountain sense—and all before they were ten—that persuaded us otherwise.

Certainly, if the very first course we organised for youngsters of ten and eleven from a school in Brixton was 'experimental', we could scarcely wait for the second group to arrive! Their sheer excitement and sense of wonder was one of the most rewarding and memorable things I have ever witnessed. I do not recall having one child on any of the courses we ran (and we held many) who had ever been away from south London before, so their reaction at seeing forests and hills, the sea and a real-life working farm for the very first time can only be imagined. I well recall one lad crying out in terror and racing back to us when his path was blocked by a sheep! He had not seen one before, and when we questioned him it emerged that he'd thought sheep were no larger than rabbits! What a thrill for him especially to visit Fron Olau farm just two days later and be given a young lamb to hold by Hugh Davies, the farmer!

On one mountain walk we had taken the children up Cwm Bychan near Beddgelert. As we reached the head of the valley and emerged on the ridge above Llyn Dinas with its striking view of Yr Aran and the Snowdon massif,

Rikki, a young coloured boy, stopped and cried out 'Isn't it big!' We looked around for what it was that had caught his attention; a big rock or waterfall perhaps? We looked in vain. 'What's big, Rikki?' we asked. 'The world!' was his reply. Later that evening, back in the Centre's lounge, we had the privilege of explaining to Rikki and his friends that indeed the world is big, because it was created by a God who is even bigger. And they believed it.

One of the most delightful things about sharing our home and our hills with these youngsters was their unspoilt openness to the idea of God and all that he had made and done for them. Scarcely any of them had come from any kind of Christian background. Quite a number knew only one parent and few had any contact with church or Sunday school. But away from the congestion and street pressure of life in Brixton they were ready to listen and learn. They would ask questions but hardly ever argue. All they saw about them bore testimony to a God who was real. Sadly, in only a few years, such openness would go, and a world of drugs and gang violence would be waiting to engulf these delightful kids we'd had for no more than a brief ten-day period.

How vital it is that whether we be parents, teachers, youth workers or just concerned friends of young people, we do all in our power to share with them the love of God and the person of the Lord Jesus Christ, before they are swallowed up by a world of ungodliness and disinterest, cynicism and downright rejection of all that we hold dear. Furthermore, if we are willing to learn something from these children, would that we as adults still felt that same sense of awe and wonder in the presence of God and the glory of his creation that young Rikki displayed! It is so easy to become over-familiar with such things and take for granted that which still ought to take our breath away.

Something we soon discovered working among the young was the important place filled by heroes in an otherwise dull, uninspiring life. One day a stranger turned up at the Mountain Centre. He had torn his wet-suit water skiing, and a local shopkeeper sent him on to us suggesting that we might be able to effect a temporary repair. I invited him in, and as I patched the damaged area for him, we talked. He told me his name was Tony Brown, and when I asked what he did for a living he informed me that he played professional football for West Bromwich Albion. 'Oh, so you're that Tony Brown', I said.

I then became aware of a growing commotion in the corridor. It so happened that we had a group of young lads from Birmingham staying with us. One of the boys a little earlier had peered inquisitively through the half-inch gap of a door left slightly ajar, and had then shared the news with his mates: 'Mike is in the dining room talking to Tony Brown!' 'Oh sure!' someone retorted, 'and the Angel Gabriel is in the staff-room playing Mike's guitar!' 'But he *is*!' cried the boy in exasperation, frustrated that none of them would believe him. There was only one way to settle the matter. A knock on the dining-room door heralded the arrival of a deputation, and I left Mr Brown with his repaired wet-suit trying to get away from a dozen or so of his devoted fans. Rather amusing, I thought, since most of them had previously declared themselves to be ardent Birmingham City supporters!

But what an opportunity that evening to tell those boys of a far greater hero—so devoted to them that he had actually died on a cross to save them from their sin and secure their friendship and loyalty not just for time but for eternity.

I share one final memory, to illustrate just how often children tend to put us adults in the shade when it comes to real trust and confidence in an all-loving and powerful God. At the time we faced something of a crisis at the Centre. The Ford 'Thames' minibus that had served us well for several years had finally reached the 'end of the road'. It was beyond reasonable repair, at a time when we had insufficient funds to purchase a replacement. One of the junior school groups from Brixton was with us, and we shared our need with them, even daring to suggest that God knew about it and could provide. That night as we put our own lads to bed and listened while they prayed, Mark's request was very straightforward: 'Lord, you know how much we need a vehicle here at the Centre. Please provide us with one so that daddy doesn't have to worry. Oh, and if you could possibly make it a long-wheelbase Landrover, that would be great—

we'd be just like the other centres.' We tried to explain to Mark that since God already knew our need it wasn't really necessary to be quite so specific, and that, in any event, Landrovers were very, very expensive and quite beyond the means of a centre like ours. Hoping that we had furthered his understanding of how to pray aright, we said good night and he settled down to sleep.

The very next morning my telephone rang. 'You won't know me,' said a voice, 'but we've followed with prayerful interest the work of the Mountain Centre for some while. I don't know what your needs are right now with regard to transport, but I'm in the process of buying a new Rangerover to replace a long-wheelbase Landrover. If you could possibly find a use for such a vehicle, we'd be delighted to give it to the Centre'! When Mark came home from school that afternoon, I told him that I owed him an apology. His faith was far greater than mine. But what a story to share that evening with those children from Brixton! What evidence of a God who says, *Before they call I will answer; while they are still speaking I will hear* (Isaiah 65:24).

Jesus told Peter by Galilee, *Feed my lambs* (John 21:15). We sought to do this and now others carry on the same work. May God keep alive the seed sown over the years, that it may yet produce a great harvest. The Bible also says, *And a little child will lead them* (Isaiah 11:6). May we as adults never be so stubborn or set in our ways that we fail to learn from those whose faith is so strong because it is so simple.

11
Sunset

'When evening comes, there will be light.'
(Zechariah 14:7)

Why is it, I have sometimes found myself asking, that God reserves His most glorious hues and breathtaking colours for the very last moments of daylight? Maybe the sun has been hidden all day; perhaps storm clouds have brooded over the hills; when suddenly, as night is about to fall, the western sky is transformed into an expansive canvas upon which is painted with extravagant brushstrokes the most wonderful shades imaginable. With little warning the display is 'turned on'. Then in less time than it takes to get a camera out of your rucksack (the voice of experience speaking!) it has faded and night descends. What a mystery! Doubtless scientists are able to explain the phenomena in terms of the specific angle of the sun and the way light is refracted as it passes through the atmosphere and so on, but nothing, surely, can detract from the fact that in the sunset God shows us something of his creative beauty and demonstrates that, compared with the work of the world's finest artists, he can do so much better.

A glorious sunset has also something else to say. At a moment when we as creatures of time think of something ending—the close of a day, light giving way to darkness—God, in the transience of the sunset, seems to be reminding us of his eternal glory. That which is so fleeting and short-lived can surely be seen as a foretaste or glimpse, albeit far off, of something truly wonderful that is yet to be. The line in John Ellerton's well-known hymn expresses it in geographical terms: *The sun that bids us rest is waking / Our brethren 'neath the western sky.* The sun that sets is not snuffed out. It is merely shining, far more brightly, in another place. The end of the day here heralds the dawn of a new day there. A simple enough thought when applied to the passage of time or the rotation of the earth, but also a profound truth when related to the death of a Christian believer.

It was the third Sunday in August 1992, and I was to preach the last of a series of sermons on *The Christian Athlete*. We had just witnessed the Barcelona Olympics and, with many young people attending our church in Colchester, it had seemed an appropriate theme to consider. But how would young folk react to this final challenge? Using Paul's words in 2 Timothy 4:6-8, I intended to speak about the end of the race; reaching the finishing line and attaining the prize. In a word: what happens when a Christian dies? The words were well known: *I am already being poured out like a drink offering, and the time has come for my departure. I have fought the good fight, I have finished the race, I have kept the faith. Now there is in store for me the crown of righteousness, which the Lord, the righteous Judge, will award to me on that day—and not only to me, but also to all who have longed for his appearing.* But how would young people, with a long life ahead of them, respond to what I had to tell them? I wanted to convey the truth that dying, for the person trusting in Christ, is not a trauma but a triumph. That it marks the end of our striving which involves sacrifice and suffering, and represents an entry into glory; the receiving of the prize from the hand of the Saviour himself. In other words, something to be viewed not with alarm, but rather anticipated with assurance and joyful hope. Not an easy concept to accept if you happen to be young and have everything to live for.

In the evening service of that same Sunday, I spoke about Onesimus, the runaway slave from Colosse. We looked at Paul's letter to Philemon, the master of Onesimus. Having been converted under Paul's ministry in Rome, the wayward slave was now prepared to go back to his owner, and although the apostle was sad to lose the young man he dearly loved, he recognised that Philemon had a greater claim upon him. And so he wrote of *my son Onesimus, who became my son while I was in chains. Formerly he was useless to you, but now he has become useful both to you and to me. I am sending him—who is my very heart—back to you. I would have liked to keep him with me . . . But . . . not . . . without your consent* (Philemon 10-14). There was no further reference to death in this sermon—that would surely have been too much for my long-suffering congregation! I simply spoke about true freedom—the freedom that is found not in trying to run away from God and his claim upon us, but rather in returning to him and becoming a true bondslave of the Lord Jesus Christ. Little did I realise, as I spoke, the way in which these very words would return to me with such significance within a very short time.

Three days later Elaine and I found ourselves sitting alone in one of the interview rooms in Llandeilo police station. We had been contacted the night before and told that Carl, our son, had been reported missing by anxious friends and that an air and land search for him would resume that morning. It had been raining heavily for several days and the rivers of the region were in flood. Carl had been out walking on his own and had failed to return that evening.

After what seemed an age, but what probably was no more than a few minutes, a police inspector came in and sat down. 'I am so very sorry,' he said, 'but some of my officers found your son's body early this morning.' He had apparently slipped in a ravine and been drowned in the swollen floodwaters of the River Cothi. He was just twenty-eight years old. We were brought a cup of tea and left to grieve in private together as we took in the news. People frequently speak in terms of disbelief and numbness at such times. Looking back on the event now, one recollection more than any other comes to my mind. It was my saying to God, with regard to Carl, *I am sending him—who is my very heart— back to you. I would have liked to keep him . . . But . . . not . . . without your consent . . . He is very dear to me but even dearer to you* (verses 12,13,14,16).

Prior to this bereavement my wife and I had each lost both our parents. We

83

Carl

were therefore familiar with the grief that accompanies the death of an elderly mother or father. But this was very different. Children expect one day to have to lose their parents, and parents equally assume that their children will survive them. The early death of a son or daughter is therefore especially distressing. Why should their life be cut short when you, a member of the previous generation, are permitted to live on? A question made all the more difficult for some, when the one who has died was involved in work of a particularly humanitarian nature. Carl had given up a career in agricultural sales, to train as a water-engineer to work specifically in the Third World. Ethiopia was 'his' country by 'adoption', and so deeply did he care for that land and its people that he insisted on working there following the fall of the Mengistu regime, when expatriates were being urged to stay away.

Following his death deeper questions were asked by those who admired the work he had been doing. Why should so needy a people lose such a valuable friend? Where is the sense in the death of such a young person with so much to give?

How grateful we were at that time to know with a great degree of assurance that God is sovereign and knows precisely what he is doing, even when his people may be completely 'in the dark'. We didn't pretend to be able to answer such questions. We didn't even try. What we did know, and what was said at a thanksgiving service for his life held in Carmarthen and attended by a great many friends who knew and loved him, was this: Whatever he may have done, in a life however short, was of little importance compared with the fact that though *very dear to us*, he was even dearer to Christ. Christ was not just the one who had called Carl to serve him; much more than this, he was the one who had saved him. In Carl's death God was not losing a servant in Ethiopia; he was receiving a son into eternal glory—someone for whom he had sent his very own Son to die on the cross of Calvary, and whom he now called to share in the everlasting blessing flowing from his work of salvation.

It was damp and overcast when we laid Carl's earthly remains to rest high

on a hillside above Llanfynydd. It was a place he loved and usually made his 'base' when in the UK. We read his favourite psalm—Psalm 62: *My soul finds rest in God alone; my salvation comes from him. He alone is my rock and my salvation; he is my fortress, I shall never be shaken . . . Find rest, O my soul, in God alone; my hope comes from him.* We also prayed and wept together. Suddenly, as if God himself was saying something to us, a gap appeared in the cloud and the sun shone through. In that moment we knew that our son was not lying buried on a Welsh hillside, but was living in an infinitely better place. Walking upon the high places for Carl now meant being in the presence of his Lord and Saviour. There was great sadness for us, for the sun had set; the 'day' of having him with us had come to its close. But we could never grieve on his account when 'sunset' for us was the dawning of a bright and glorious day for him.

What a blessed and privileged people we are, who know and trust the Saviour! To be able to face human sorrow and loss not as others who have no hope, but in serenity anticipating with God-given assurance a time when we also *shall ever be with the Lord* . . . UPON THE HIGH PLACES (1 Thessalonians 4:13,17; Isaiah 58:14 AV).

'The Delectable Mountains'

They went then till they came to the *Delectable Mountains*; which mountains belong to the Lord of that Hill, of which we have spoken before; so they went up to the mountains, to behold the Gardens and Orchards, the Vineyards, and Fountains of water; where also they drank and washed themselves, and did freely eat of the vineyards. Now there was on the tops of those mountains, Shepherds feeding their Flocks, and they stood by the Highway side. The Pilgrims therefore went to them, and leaning upon their staves, (as is common with weary Pilgrims, when they stand to talk with any by the way) they asked, *Whose Delectable Mountains are these? And whose be the Sheep that feed upon them?*

Shepherd: These mountains are *Emmanuel's Land*, and they are within sight of his City; and the Sheep also are his, and he laid down his Life for them.

John Bunyan, *Pilgrim's Progress,* Part I.

UPON HIGH PLACES

UPON HIGH PLACES

UPON HIGH PLACES

UPON HIGH PLACES